TO MY HUSBAND, MIKE, WHO HAS ALWAYS
BELIEVED IN MY "IMPOSSIBLE" DREAMS
—A. B.

THIS BOOK IS DEDICATED TO ALL THE
YOUNG WOMEN COMPETING TO BLAZE THEIR
OWN TRAIL AND BREAK THEIR OWN ICE.
—C. F. P.

SIMON & SCHUSTER BOOKS FOR YOUNG READERS
An imprint of Simon & Schuster Children's Publishing Division
1230 Avenue of the Americas, New York, New York 10020
Text copyright © 2020 by Angie Bullaro
Illustrations copyright © 2020 by C. F. Payne
All rights reserved, including the right of reproduction in whole or in part in any form.
SIMON & SCHUSTER BOOKS FOR YOUNG READERS is a trademark of Simon & Schuster, Inc.
For information about special discounts for bulk purchases, please contact Simon & Schuster
Special Sales at 1-866-506-1949 or business@simonandschuster.com.
The Simon & Schuster Speakers Bureau can bring authors to your live event.
For more information or to book an event, contact the Simon & Schuster Speakers Bureau
at 1-866-248-3049 or visit our website at www.simonspeakers.com.
Book design by Lucy Ruth Cummins
The text for this book was set in Adobe Garamond Pro.
The illustrations for this book were rendered in acrylics and colored pencils.
Manufactured in China
0620 SCP
First Edition
2 4 6 8 10 9 7 5 3 1
CIP data for this book is available from the Library of Congress.
ISBN 978-1-5344-2557-6
ISBN 978-1-5344-2558-3 (eBook)

BREAKING THE ICE

WRITTEN BY ANGIE BULLARO
ILLUSTRATED BY C. F. PAYNE
WITH AN AFTERWORD BY MANON RHÉAUME

A Paula Wiseman Book
Simon & Schuster Books for Young Readers
New York London Toronto Sydney New Delhi

anon's fingers itched to hold a hockey stick. Her brothers flew across the ice, while Manon stood on the sidelines watching.

Swish. Swoosh. Skates glided from side to side. *Shhhwoop.* A sudden stop. *Whoosh.* The stick cut through the air. *Ker-chunk.* The stick hit the puck, sending it down the ice. Manon imagined blocking the puck.

"I wish I could play on the team too," Manon said with a sigh. In 1977 in her hometown of Lac-Beauport, Quebec, Canada (and everywhere else in the world), hockey was a "boy's" sport.

But that was all about to change.

Shortly after Manon's fifth birthday, the team her dad coached needed a goalie for their first game.

Manon took a deep breath and whispered, "Dad, I can play goalie." Her parents stared at her with eyes as big as hockey pucks.

"Play goalie?" Dad said.

"Hockey?!" Mom exclaimed. "That's for boys."

"But she plays all the time with us in the backyard," her brothers chimed in.

"And they always make me play goalie," Manon said. "Pleeeease! I can do it."

It was a crazy idea. Manon didn't even own hockey skates. She had never practiced with the team. And she would be the only girl in the league. But the team needed a goalie, and Manon wanted a chance.

On the day of the game, Manon didn't worry that she had never played on a team before. All she cared about was finally being in the game. She raced toward the ice.

"Manon, wait!" Dad called out. He pulled a goalie mask out of his bag and handed it to her.

"Why do I have to put on the mask now?" Manon asked.

"People aren't ready to see a girl play on a boys' team. Not yet," Dad said. "But don't let that stop you. You can do anything you put your mind to."

Manon did as he said and then skated to the goalie net. No one could see there was a girl's face behind the mask.

Manon didn't realize she was about to change history. She was too busy enjoying the game.

Playing goalie was much trickier than Manon had imagined. Goalie equipment was heavy and bulky, making it difficult to stand up on her skates. And the puck stung worse than a bee when it hit a part of her body not covered by pads.

But none of that compared to the feeling of blocking the puck from entering the goal. With each save, her team erupted in cheers. They were ecstatic that the new player could stop a shot, even if she was a girl.

Three things were clear after that game. One, Manon was not afraid of the puck slamming into her. Two, she needed to practice if she wanted to get better. Three, she loved playing goalie more than playing with her toys, skiing, figure skating, ballet, or anything else.

The next week Manon joined the team her dad coached. She was the only girl in the entire league, which didn't matter when she was young. The kids came to the rink already dressed and left with their gear still on. Manon didn't have to worry about changing in a separate locker room or feeling different from the rest of the team. Sometimes the other teams and parents didn't even know there was a girl under all that equipment. But as she grew older, being the only girl started to matter more and more.

Kids from other teams taunted her. "Girls play dolls, not hockey."

Parents complained. "She's taking our son's spot on the team."

Coaches shook their heads. "No girl will ever play on *my* team."

But Manon believed in herself even when others doubted her. She worked her hardest to prove she belonged in the game.

Nothing could stop Manon from playing hockey. Not ice spraying in her face, pucks crashing into her mask, or players plowing her over.

"You have to work harder and be tougher than the boys," Dad said. Manon arrived early and stayed late after practice. She played with bruised arms and pulled muscles. She skated on the ice until it was too dark to see the pucks.

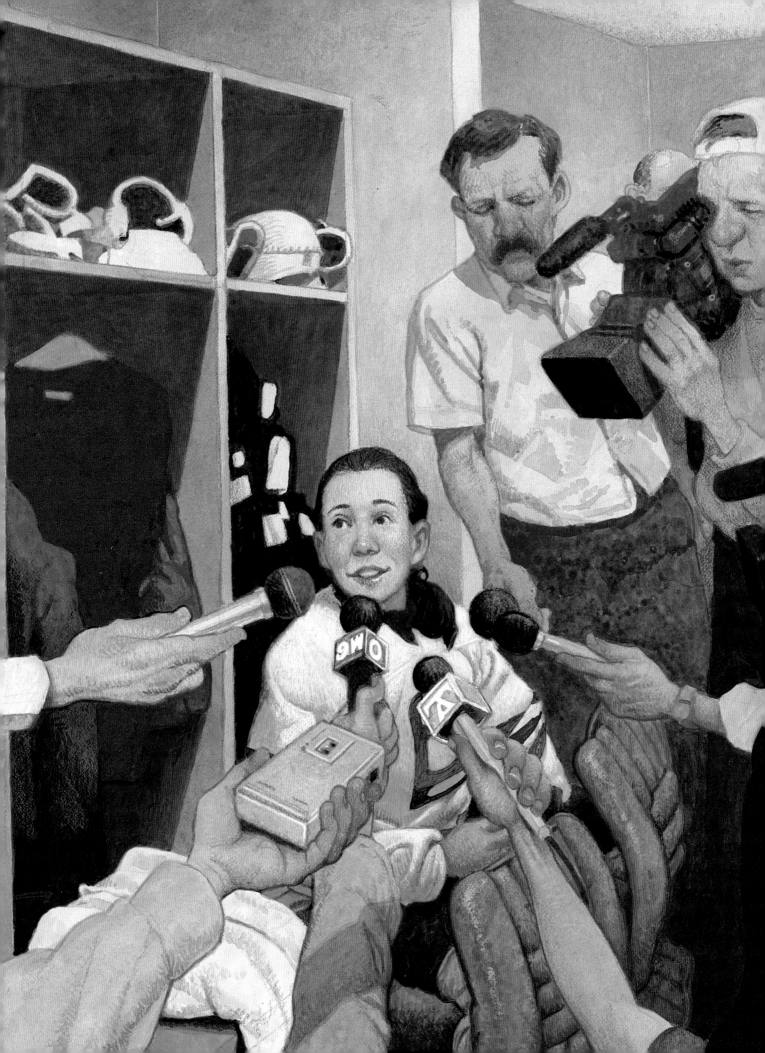

In 1984, several years after her first game, Manon made history when she played in the prestigious Quebec International Pee-Wee Hockey Tournament. Never had a girl played in the tournament. In fact, the rules had to be changed to allow her to enter.

Dozens of reporters crowded around the shy, eleven-year-old girl who had just broken the "rules." They couldn't believe a girl, and one so small, could stop such hard shots.

"Manon, do you think girls could play hockey at a higher level?" one reporter asked. In a voice just above a whisper, Manon replied, "One day, a woman will make the National Hockey League. If no one prevents her."

From that moment on, reporters followed Manon to her games. She didn't want the extra attention. She just wanted to play hockey.

By the time Manon was a teenager, she was one of the top goalies in her age group. But coaches still cut her from the best teams simply because she was a girl. It was unfair and made her angry.

Manon could have quit. But she didn't.

Instead she continued playing her best, and slowly her luck started to change. In 1991, Gaston Drapeau, coach for a Quebec Major Junior Hockey League team, saw how talented Manon was and asked her to be the third-string goalie on his team.

Months of practicing passed by before Manon got to play. During one of the last games of the season, the starting goalie was injured and the backup goalie blew a big lead. Coach Drapeau decided it was time to take a chance with Manon and put her in a game.

The crowd gave her a standing ovation as she skated to the net. She was a bundle of nerves. Luckily, she was covered in goalie gear, so no one could see her shaking. Once she was in position, all of her fears melted away. In front of the net was where she felt the most alive and the most confident. The fans went wild every time she blocked a shot. She was playing her best ever until a hard shot slammed into her mask. The mask cracked, cutting a deep gouge into the side of Manon's face. She was forced to leave the game to get stitches. It was her first and last game in the Major Junior Hockey League.

Less than a year later, when she was twenty years old, something extraordinary happened. Phil Esposito, general manager of a new NHL team called the Tampa Bay Lightning, saw footage of Manon playing during the Quebec Major Junior Hockey League game. He was impressed with what he saw.

"That goalie has talent," Phil said to his scout. "Invite him to the camp for tryouts."

After the game was finished, Manon took off her mask. Phil paused the tape and peered closely at the goalie. "A girl!" he exclaimed.

Phil could have changed his mind. But he didn't.

In 1992 there was not a professional hockey team for women. And no woman had ever played a game in any of the top four male professional sports leagues in America—not hockey, football, baseball, or basketball. Manon would have to pave her own way and that made her nervous. Everyone would be watching her.

No one could believe a girl was going to a professional tryout, not even Manon.

What if I can't do it? she thought. She closed her eyes and imagined herself blocking the winning goal. A smile skated onto her face.

"Are you sure you want to go?" her mom asked. "You'll be playing against men, not boys."

"I need to know how far I can go," Manon replied. "This is a once-in-a-lifetime chance, and I don't want to look back and wonder what might have happened." Manon's love of the game was stronger than her fear, so she packed her bags and left for Florida.

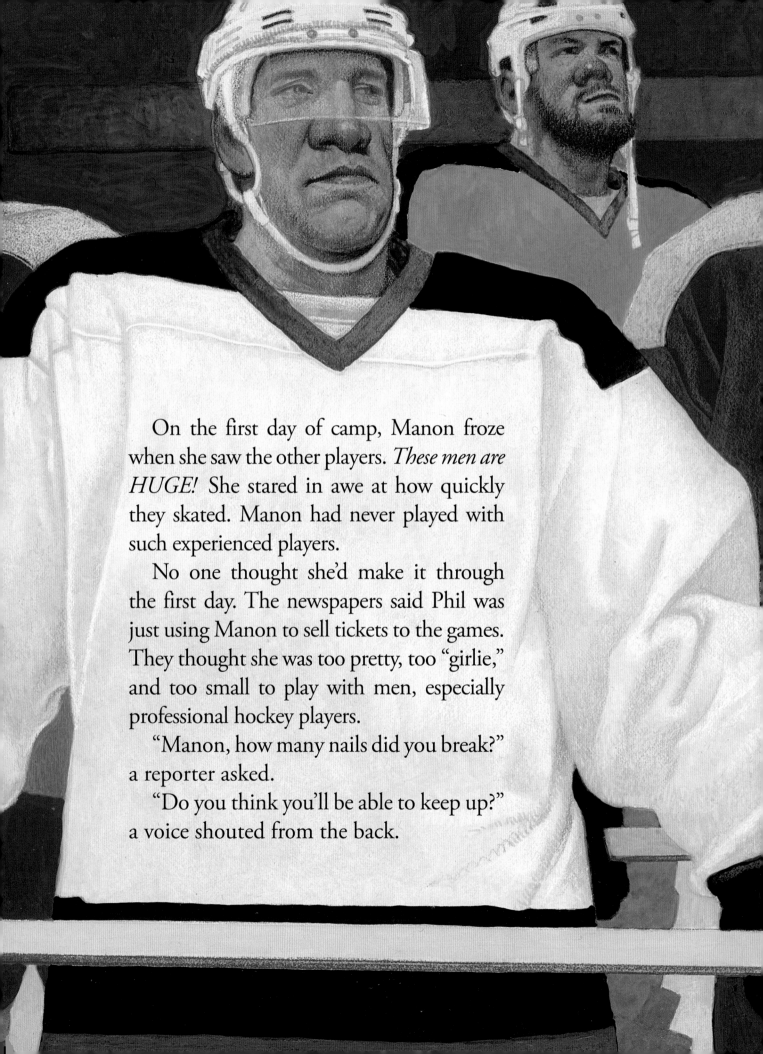

On the first day of camp, Manon froze when she saw the other players. *These men are HUGE!* She stared in awe at how quickly they skated. Manon had never played with such experienced players.

No one thought she'd make it through the first day. The newspapers said Phil was just using Manon to sell tickets to the games. They thought she was too pretty, too "girlie," and too small to play with men, especially professional hockey players.

"Manon, how many nails did you break?" a reporter asked.

"Do you think you'll be able to keep up?" a voice shouted from the back.

Manon bit her lip. She had years of practice blocking out negative comments. She knew the only way to quiet their doubts was to focus on the game and play her best.

The first day came and went, but Manon survived. By the end of the week it was time for the first round of cuts. Manon paced inside her locker room, waiting to be sent home like most of the other rookies. Her heart raced faster than a hundred-mile-per-hour puck. Instead of telling Manon she would go home, Phil said, "Keep up the great work!" Manon was ecstatic. She had another week to play.

When the reporters found out Manon was still at the camp, they tried even harder to cut her down. "She's a publicity stunt," one reporter wrote.

Manon didn't care if that was true or not. All her life, people had told her she couldn't play because she was a girl. Now someone had told her she *could* play because she was a girl. She was going to make the most of the chance she had been given. She would finally know just how far she could go.

After practices the other players relaxed in the warm southern sun. But Manon had to rush off to dozens of news interviews, press conferences, and photo shoots. Some nights she was so exhausted, her knees wobbled beneath her. Between practices and the publicity, Manon hardly had time to sleep.

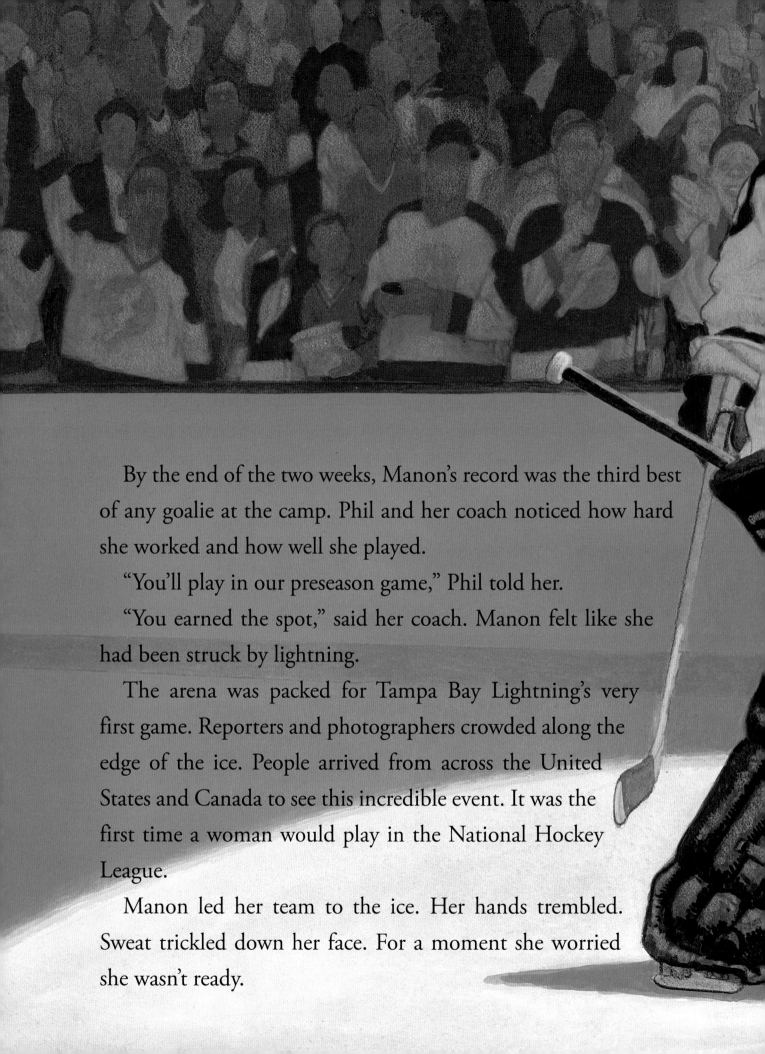

By the end of the two weeks, Manon's record was the third best of any goalie at the camp. Phil and her coach noticed how hard she worked and how well she played.

"You'll play in our preseason game," Phil told her.

"You earned the spot," said her coach. Manon felt like she had been struck by lightning.

The arena was packed for Tampa Bay Lightning's very first game. Reporters and photographers crowded along the edge of the ice. People arrived from across the United States and Canada to see this incredible event. It was the first time a woman would play in the National Hockey League.

Manon led her team to the ice. Her hands trembled. Sweat trickled down her face. For a moment she worried she wasn't ready.

As soon as Manon stepped onto the ice, though, her fear melted away. The crowd became a blur. The noise faded. Now she wasn't nervous. She was focused. She was where she belonged.

The people in the stands jumped to their feet and cheered wildly when Manon skated to the net. Her teammates tapped her on her shoulder pads. Her coach nodded his approval. Finally, they all believed in her.

Manon pulled down her mask and did what she loved best.

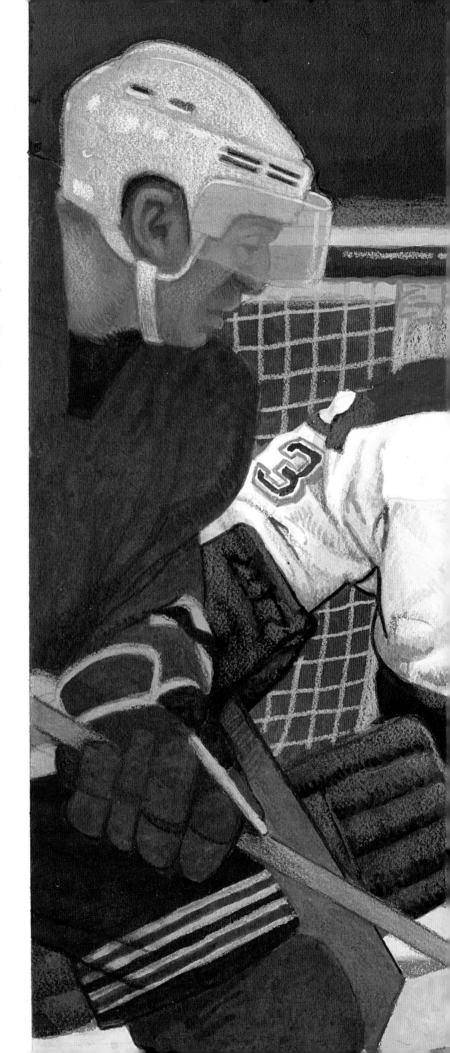

AFTERWORD

On September 23, 1992, I made history as the first woman to play in an NHL game, with the Tampa Bay Lightning. I was young and did not realize the impact my story would have on people. I was just playing the sport I grew up with and loved more than anything. It's crazy to think that twenty-eight years later I am still the only female to have played a game, not only in the NHL, but in any of the four major North American sports leagues.

When I agreed to attend the Tampa Bay Lightning training camp, my goal was to be able to participate in the highest level of hockey. I had no idea my life would change like it did. A lot of people tried to convince me to not attend the camp. They thought I would embarrass myself or that I was just invited because I was a girl. But I didn't let their negative attitudes and comments stop me from following my dream. I didn't want to live my life with regret.

So many times throughout my life people had said no to me because I was a girl. If this time being a girl was going to work to my advantage, then I wanted to take that opportunity. No matter the reason they invited me, I still had to prove myself and to perform at the highest level. I had to face those shots every day and block them.

It's amazing to see how far women's hockey has grown since the time I started. Now there are female leagues where girls can play hockey from a young age. Girls can earn full scholarships to play college hockey and go on to play pro hockey in a women's league. They can even represent their country in the Olympic games.

Looking back at my accomplishments, the most satisfying part is that my story inspires people. The best advice I can give you from my journey is to follow your dreams despite the odds or setbacks. Don't let "no" stop you. With hard work and passion you can achieve anything you put your mind to.

—Manon Rhéaume

TIME LINE

1972 – February 24, Manon Rhéaume is born in Lac-Beauport, Quebec, in Canada.

1977 – Manon plays goalie in her first hockey game. Her father is the coach and her brother also plays on the team. She's the only girl on the team and in the league.

1984 – Manon becomes the first female to play in the Quebec International Pee-Wee Hockey Tournament. The tournament rules had to be changed to allow her participation. Many legendary hockey players competed in this tournament when they were younger, such as Wayne Gretzky, Guy Lafleur, Daniel Bouchard, Marcel Dionne, and Gilbert Perreault.

1984 – The Quebec newspaper *Le Progrès-Dimanche* prints an article with this quote from Manon: "One day, a woman will make the National Hockey League. If no one prevents her."

1991 – Manon plays a game with the Quebec Major Junior Hockey League (QMJHL) team the Draveur's. She is the first woman to play in the QMJHL and at a level this high.

1992 – Manon's female hockey team in Sherbrooke, Quebec, wins the Quebec championship and the bronze medal at the Canadian championship.

1992 – Manon plays with the Canadian National Women's Hockey Team in Finland at the International Ice Hockey Federation's Women's World Championship. Canada wins the gold Medal and Manon is named the best goalie for the All Tournament team.

1992 – Manon plays one period in the Tampa Bay Lightning's preseason game against the St. Louis Blues. She is the first woman to play a game in either the National Hockey League, National Basketball Association, National Football League, or Major League Baseball.

1992- The International Hockey League's Atlanta Knights signs Manon to their team.

1993 – Manon played another preseason game with the Tampa Bay Lightning against the Boston Bruins.

1994 – Manon again plays with the Canadian National Women's Hockey Team at the International Ice Hockey Federation's Women's World Championship, this time in Lake Placid, New York. Again, her team wins gold and she is named an All-Star as top goaltender.

1994 – Manon joins the Roller Hockey International League as part of the New Jersey Rockin' Rollers team. She is the first woman to win a game in professional roller hockey.

1998 – The first year women's ice hockey is an Olympic sport. Manon plays with Team Canada at the Olympics in Nagano, Japan. They win the silver medal.

FUN FACTS ABOUT MANON

Manon was the first girl to play in the prestigious Quebec International Pee-Wee Hockey Tournament in Canada. The rules had to be changed in order for her to play. She paved the way for future girl ice-hockey players to also play in the tournament.

She was the first female to play in a Quebec Major Junior Hockey League game. She played goalie for seventeen minutes against the Granby Bisons. She was taken out of the game when a puck crashed into her face, cracking her mask and causing her to need multiple stitches.

She was the first woman to ever play a game in any of the major professional North American sports leagues. She was also the first woman to play in the International Hockey League, a minor league of the NHL.

She spent five years in professional minor leagues, playing for six different teams and appearing in twenty-four games.

She has two sons, Dylan and Dakoda, who both play hockey and aspire to play in the NHL. If either of her sons plays in the NHL, it will be the first time in the history of the four major professional North American leagues that a mother and son will play in the same league. Dylan is also a goalie, so he would be playing the same position as his mother.

She holds both U.S. and Canadian citizenship. Her parents still live in Quebec, Canada, but Manon and her sons live in Michigan.

Growing up, Manon wasn't just great at hockey, she was also a stellar student. She earned top marks in all of her classes.

"IT'S NEVER BEEN EASY. BUT I ALWAYS WANTED TO PLAY HOCKEY. I LOVE HOCKEY. I'D RATHER PLAY HOCKEY THAN ANYTHING ELSE. IF YOU HAVE THAT KIND OF DESIRE, I THINK YOU CAN ACHIEVE WHAT YOU WANT TO ACHIEVE."

—MANON RHÉAUME

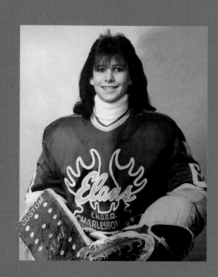